LIFE CYCLES

Anita Ganeri

Heinemann
LIBRARY

www.heinemann.co.uk
Visit our website to find out more information about Heinemann Library books.

To order:
☎ Phone 44 (0) 1865 888066
🖹 Send a fax to 44 (0) 1865 314091
🖥 Visit the Heinemann Bookshop at www.heinemann.co.uk to browse our catalogue and order online.

First published in Great Britain by Heinemann Library, Halley Court, Jordan Hill, Oxford OX2 8EJ a division of Reed Educational and Professional Publishing Ltd. Heinemann is a registered trademark of Reed Educational & Professional Publishing Ltd.

OXFORD MELBOURNE AUCKLAND
JOHANNESBURG BLANTYRE GABORONE
IBADAN PORTSMOUTH (NH) USA CHICAGO

Designed by Celia Floyd
Illustrations by Alan Fraser
Originated by Dot Gradations
Printed in Hong Kong/China

ISBN 0 431 10923 0 (hardback)   ISBN 0 431 10930 3 (paperback)
06 05 04 03 02 01   06 05 04 03 02 01
10 9 8 7 6 5 4 3 2   10 9 8 7 6 5 4 3 2 1

British Library Cataloguing in Publication Data

Ganeri, Anita
  Life cycles. – (Living things)
  1. Life cycles (Biology) – Juvenile literature
  I. Title
  571.8

Acknowledgements

The Publishers would like to thank the following for permission to reproduce photographs:

Corbis: pg.24; *NHPA*: MI Walker pg.4, GI Bernard pg.5, pg.7, pg.13, ANT pg.5, Brian Hawkes pg.8, Stephen Dalton pg.12, pg.13, pg.19, NA Callow pg.13, Ron Fotheringham pg.13, Stephen Krasemann pg.14, pg.15, Pavel German pg.21, Yves Lanceau pg.26, Gerard Lacz pg.27; *Oxford Scientific Films*: Colin Milkins pg.15, Mark Deeble & Victoria Stone pg.16, Zig Leszczynski pg.20, Doug Allan pg.22, Daniel J Cox pg.23; *Planet Earth Pictures*: Doug Perrine pg.16; *Robert Harding Picture Library*: Raj Kamal pg.11.

Cover photograph reproduced with permission of Oxford Scientific Films.

Every effort has been made to contact copyright holders of any material reproduced in this book. Any omissions will be rectified in subsequent printings if notice is given to the Publisher.

Any words appearing in the text in bold, **like this**, are explained in the glossary.

Contents

Introduction

The six books in this series explore the world of living things. *Life Cycles* looks at the different stages in a living thing's life, from birth through to death. New living things are born all the time to replace those that die. Then the cycle of life can begin again.

Living and dying

A life cycle describes the stages in a living thing's life. It is born, grows and eventually dies. While it is alive and strong, it makes more of itself to replace those that die. This is called **reproduction**. Living things reproduce in two main ways. These are called **asexual** reproduction and **sexual** reproduction.

Asexual reproduction

Some living things reproduce by splitting in two. Sometimes part of the parent splits off to make a new living thing. The new living thing looks exactly like its parent. This is called asexual reproduction. It is the simplest form of reproduction.

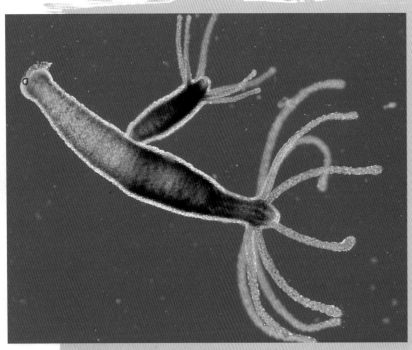

A new hydra splitting off its parent.

Hydra reproduction

A hydra is a tiny animal with tentacles. It lives in ponds and reproduces asexually. A group of **cells** grows on the hydra's body. The growth looks like a small bud. It grows tentacles and then splits off to form a brand-new animal.

Sexual reproduction

Many living things use sexual reproduction. The female makes a special cell called an **egg cell**. The male makes a cell called a **sperm**. The two cells join to make a new cell. This is called **fertilization**. The new cell grows into a new living thing.

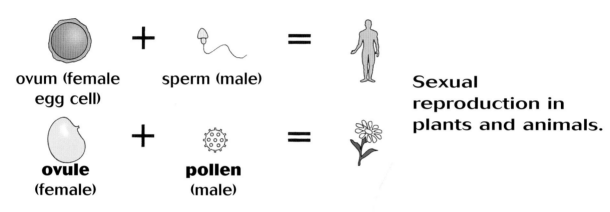

ovum (female egg cell)   **+**   sperm (male)   **=**

ovule (female)   **+**   **pollen** (male)   **=**

Sexual reproduction in plants and animals.

A strawberry plant can reproduce asexually by putting out a new stem which will grow into a new plant. It can also reproduce sexually from seeds.

Fertilization

In some animals, fertilization happens inside the female's body. In other animals, it happens outside. A female crab lays her egg cells in the water. Then the male fertilizes them with his sperm. The fertilized eggs are washed out to sea to hatch.

A female crab laying her eggs in the sea.

5

Flowering plants

A flowering plant is a plant that has flowers. Flowering plants grow from seeds. The flower is where the seeds are made. Later the seeds will grow into new plants. The flower has male parts and female parts. The male parts make **pollen**. The female parts make **ovules**. The pollen and ovule must join together to make a seed. This is called **pollination**.

Inside a buttercup flower

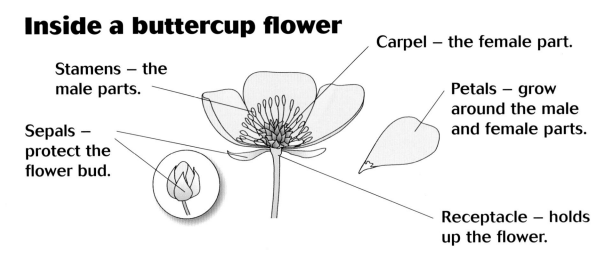

Stamens – the male parts.

Carpel – the female part.

Petals – grow around the male and female parts.

Sepals – protect the flower bud.

Receptacle – holds up the flower.

A carpel is made of an ovary, a stigma and a style. Inside the ovary are tiny ovules. The stigma catches the pollen. The style joins the stigma to the ovary.

Stigma

Ovary

Style

Ovule

A stamen is made of a filament and an anther. The anther makes pollen. The filament holds the anther up.

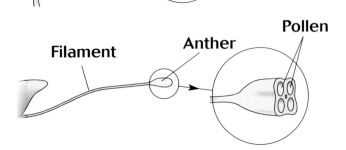

Filament

Anther

Pollen

Pollination

To make a seed, the pollen must reach the ovule. The anther splits open and shakes out millions of tiny pollen grains. A pollen grain lands on the stigma. Then it grows a long tube into the ovary. The pollen joins the ovule. Then a seed begins to grow. Some plants can pollinate themselves. Other plants need pollen from another plant.

Did you know?

Some flowering plants only live for one year. They grow and make flowers and seeds very quickly. Then the plants die. Other plants live for many years. But they die down each winter and shoot up again in spring.

Colours and smells

Flowering plants need help to spread their pollen. Some plants use the wind to carry pollen from one plant to another. Other plants are pollinated by insects, birds and bats. These plants often have colourful, sweet-smelling flowers to attract animals to them. The animals visit the flowers and drink their sweet **nectar**. As they drink, their bodies get covered in pollen.

A honeybee on a flower.

From seeds to plants

Once a flower has been **pollinated**, a seed begins to grow. Inside a seed are the parts that will grow into a new plant and a store of food for the new plant to use. Seeds grow inside fruits. A fruit may be a nut, a berry or a pod. The fruit protects the seed. The seeds need to be scattered to find a good place to grow. Then they grow into new plants. This is called **germination**.

Parts of a seed.

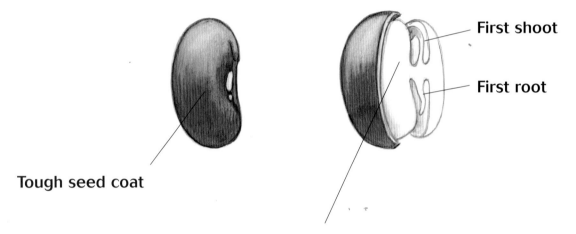

First shoot

First root

Tough seed coat

Young plant's food store

Scattering seeds

If all a plant's seeds grew in the same place, it would soon get too crowded. The seeds need to be scattered to grow. Some seeds are scattered by the wind. Some seeds are scattered by birds. Birds eat fruits. The seeds inside the fruits pass through the birds' bodies and fall to the ground in their droppings.

How a seed grows.

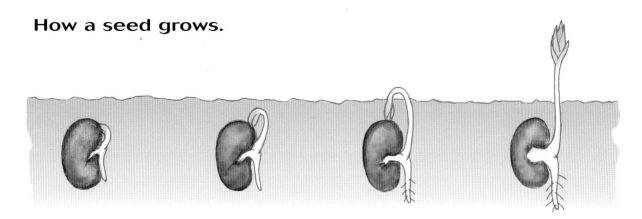

1 The seed uses its food store to grow.

2 The seed grows its first root. The root sucks up water and **minerals** from the ground.

3 The seed grows its first shoot.

4 The seed grows its first leaves. Now it begins to make its own food by **photosynthesis**.

Conifer life cycles

Conifers grow cones instead of flowers and fruit. Their seeds grow inside the cones. The cones start off soft and green. They turn brown and hard to protect the seeds. In warm, dry weather, the cones open and drop the seeds. The wind blows the seeds away.

Pine cones.

Growing from spores

Some plants do not grow from seeds. These plants grow from **spores**. Spores look like tiny specks of dust. Plants release millions of spores into the air. The wind carries the spores away. If they land in a good place, they grow into new plants.

Fern life cycles

Ferns make spores underneath their leaves. The spores make patterns that look like tiny patches of rust. When the spores are ripe, the fern releases them into the air. A spore does not grow straight into a new fern. It has another change to go through first.

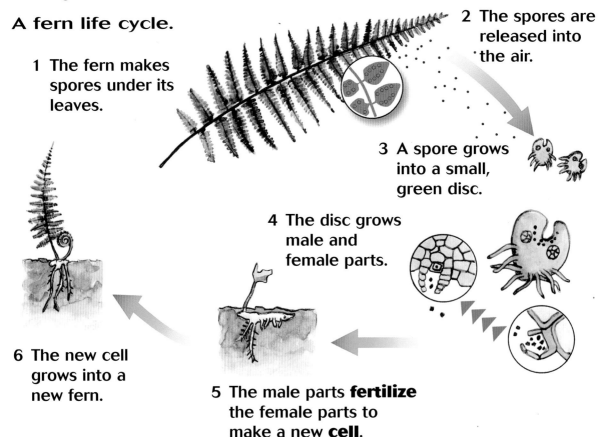

A fern life cycle.

1 The fern makes spores under its leaves.

2 The spores are released into the air.

3 A spore grows into a small, green disc.

4 The disc grows male and female parts.

6 The new cell grows into a new fern.

5 The male parts **fertilize** the female parts to make a new **cell**.

Fungi life cycle

Toadstools and mushrooms are fungi. Fungi are not plants or animals. They belong to another group of living things. But new fungi grow from spores, like ferns. Toadstools grow spores on tiny ridges called **gills**. The gills grow under the toadstool's **cap**. The cap protects the spores from rain and the stalk holds the spores up to the wind.

Did you know?

Giant puffballs are fungi that look large melons. They make an incredible 70,000,000,000,000 spores. They puff the spores out in clouds. The wind blows the spores away.

A giant puffball.

How a toadstool grows.

1 A spore lands in the ground and starts to grow.

2 It grows into a clump of threads called a button.

3 The button grows upwards. It splits to show a stalk and a cap.

4 The stalk grows taller. Gills grow under the cap. The gills make spores.

Insect life cycles

Most young insects hatch from eggs. But they look nothing like their parents. First, they have to go through some amazing changes as they grow up. These changes are called **metamorphosis**. An adult insect may have a very short life. For example, a mayfly only lives for one day. But in that time, the insect must find a **mate** so that it can make eggs.

Amazing changes

All insects change as they grow up. For some insects, this happens in four stages. These are the egg, the **larva**, the **pupa** and the adult. Butterflies, moths and beetles go through these changes. Opposite you can see how a large white butterfly grows from an egg into an adult.

Locust life cycle

Locusts start life as eggs. But when they hatch they look like tiny adults. Locusts grow in three stages. These are the egg, the **nymph** and the adult.

How a locust grows.

1 The locust lays her eggs in the sand.

2 Tiny nymphs hatch from the eggs. They look like adults but do not have wings.

3 The nymphs feed and grow. They have to grow bigger coats as they get bigger. The old coats split and fall off.

4 Finally, the nymph becomes an adult, complete with wings (see picture).

Butterfly life cycle

1 The butterfly lays her eggs on a cabbage leaf. The eggs take about a week to hatch.

2 The eggs hatch into caterpillars (butterfly larvae). The caterpillars eat the leaves and grow.

3 Each caterpillar spins a silk case around its body. It is now a pupa. It hangs under a leaf.

4 Inside the pupa, the caterpillar's body changes. It turns into an adult butterfly.

5 Finally, the pupa splits open and the butterfly comes out.

Did you know?

Most insects lay their eggs and leave them. But earwigs are caring parents. The female lays her eggs in a hole in the ground. She guards the eggs and keeps them clean until they hatch.

Spiders and scorpions

Like insects, spiders and scorpions lay eggs. The young are called **nymphs**. When they hatch, they look like tiny versions of their parents. They have to shed their skins several times before they reach adult size. Ticks and mites are related to spiders. Some ticks and mites only live for a few weeks while some spiders live for 30 years.

A tick.

Scorpion dance

Before they **mate**, scorpions do an amazing dance. The male waves his pincers in the air and taps his feet on the ground. Then the male and female link their pincers. They dance to and fro, sometimes for hours on end.

Young scorpions

A female scorpion lays up to 95 eggs. The eggs hatch almost at once. Then the baby scorpions climb on to their mother's back. They cling on with their pincers and legs. Their mother carries them about until they are old enough to look after themselves.

Spider eggs

Many spiders lay huge numbers of eggs. This is to make sure that some survive. Many are eaten by other animals. Some spiders lay up to 2500 eggs at a time. The eggs are protected in a silk purse.

Spider care

The female wolf spider spins a silk purse for her eggs. The purse is fixed to her body. When she goes out hunting, she drags the purse with her. When the baby spiders hatch, their mother carries them on her back for safety.

A wolf spider carrying her babies.

Did you know?

Horseshoe crabs are not real crabs. They are related to spiders and scorpions. They live in warm seas. But every spring, at high tide, hundreds of thousands of crabs come ashore. They lay their eggs in the sand. When the young crabs hatch, they dash to the sea. Many are eaten by sea birds.

Horseshoe crabs laying their eggs.

Fish life cycles

Most fish lay eggs. The female lays her eggs in the water. Then the male covers them with **sperm**. Many eggs are eaten by birds and fish. So some fish lay huge numbers of eggs to make sure that some survive. Other fish, including some sharks, give birth to live babies that look like their

parents. Once the baby shark has been born, its mother swims off and leaves it to look after itself. Some sharks lay eggs that have tendrils for holding on to coral or seaweed until they hatch.

A baby shark being born.

Did you know?

Some fish take great care of their young. A female mouthbrooder fish keeps her eggs in her mouth for around ten days until they hatch. Even then, the young fish stay close to their mother. They swim back into her mouth if there is danger nearby.

A mouthbrooder fish with her young.

Salmon life cycle

Most fish live either in the sea or in **fresh** water. But salmon live in both. A salmon hatches and dies in the same river. In between, it makes an amazing journey. Here you can follow a salmon's life cycle.

1 A female salmon lays her eggs in a river. Several males **fertilize** them.

2 The eggs hatch into tiny fish. They carry a supply of food.

6 Then the adults die and the life cycle begins again.

3 The tiny fish grow bigger.

4 After one to five years in the river, the fish swim out to sea. They travel thousands of kilometres. Their journey lasts for several years. At sea, they feed and grow.

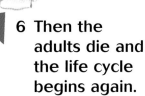

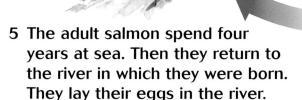

5 The adult salmon spend four years at sea. Then they return to the river in which they were born. They lay their eggs in the river.

17

Amphibian life cycles

Amphibians are animals such as frogs, toads, newts and salamanders. Adult amphibians live on land but they lay their eggs in the water. When the young hatch, they have tails for swimming and they breathe through **gills**, like fish. Later, they grow lungs and legs for living on land. These changes are called **metamorphosis**. The name amphibian means 'two lives'. This is because amphibians live both on land and water.

Frog life cycle

Here you can see the life cycle of a frog.

1 In spring, adult frogs travel to the pond.

2 The female lays her eggs and the male **fertilizes** them. The eggs float near the surface of the pond. They are covered in jelly to protect them.

3 About two weeks later, the eggs hatch. Tiny **tadpoles** come out. They live in the water and breathe through gills.

4 Over the next few months, the tadpoles grow lungs and legs. They look more like tiny frogs.

5 The little frogs spend more time on land. Then they leave the pond for good. It takes three years for them to reach adult size.

Caring parents

Some amphibians look after their eggs very carefully. Male midwife toads wind strings of eggs around their back legs. They carry the eggs around with them. When the eggs are ready to hatch, the male goes to the pond. He lowers his back legs into the water. Then the tadpoles swim away.

Did you know?
The axolotl is a salamander from Mexico. It starts life as an egg, then a tadpole. But it never grows into an adult. To complete their life cycle, the axolotl needs a **chemical** called **iodine**. But there is no iodine where they live.

An axolotl.

Reptile life cycles

Snakes, turtles, tortoises, crocodiles and lizards are reptiles. Most reptiles lay eggs on land, in nests made of mud or leaves, or in holes dug in sand or soil. The eggs have thick shells to stop them drying out. Lizards and snakes lay eggs with leathery shells. Turtles and crocodiles lay eggs with hard shells. Inside an egg is a store of food, water and **oxygen** for the baby reptile to live on. Some reptiles, such as some snakes, produce live babies.

Snake life cycle

Here is the life cycle of an American corn snake.

1 The female lays her eggs in a tree stump.

2 Inside its egg, the baby snake feeds and grows for about eight weeks.

3 The baby snake cuts a slit in the eggshell. It uses a special sharp spike on its nose. This is called an egg-tooth.

4 It spends the day in its shell, poking its head in and out.

5 Next day, the baby slithers out of its egg.

6 A few days later, it sheds its old skin and grows a new, bigger skin. It does this several more times before it reaches adult size.

A corn snake with her eggs.

Crocodile care

A crocodile lays her eggs in a hole near the water's edge. She covers them with plants and soil. She guards the nest for three months, until the eggs hatch. When she hears a squeaking noise coming from the eggs, she digs them up. The baby crocodiles break out of their shells. Then their mother picks them up in her mouth and carries them to the water.

Dash to the sea

Sea turtles live in the ocean. But they come ashore to lay their eggs. Some turtles swim thousands of kilometres to find a suitable beach. The females lay their eggs in holes in the sand. Then they go back to the sea. The baby turtles hatch, then dash to the sea. Many are eaten by crabs and birds on the way.

A green turtle.

Did you know?
The reptile that lives the longest is the huge Marion's tortoise from the Seychelles. A male tortoise that died in 1918 was believed to be 152 years old. This is also the longest-lived land animal ever.

Bird life cycles

Birds lay eggs with hard shells. Many birds build nests as safe places to lay their eggs. One parent sits on the eggs until they hatch. This keeps the eggs warm so that the **chicks** grow properly. Some eggs take about ten days to hatch. Other eggs take up to two months. Birds are caring parents. They stay with their chicks and feed them until they can fly away. But some chicks leave the nest as soon as they hatch.

Birds' eggs

A bird's egg contains everything a baby bird needs to survive. The hard shell protects the chick. The shell is covered in tiny holes to let **oxygen** in. The white of the egg contains water. The yellow **yolk** is a supply of nourishing food.

An emperor penguin with his egg.

Penguin parents

Emperor penguins live in icy Antarctica. The female lays a single egg. Then she swims off to sea to feed. The male holds the egg between his feet. He spends three months in the freezing cold, until the egg hatches. Then the female returns to feed the chick.

Learning to fly

Some birds grow up very quickly. Young birds such as ducklings leave the nest almost straight away. But others, such as pigeons and woodpeckers, are blind and need to be looked after. Their parents have to bring them food. A baby mallee fowl can fly one day after it hatches. But some birds learn to fly more slowly. It takes a wandering albatross chick about nine months before it makes its first flight from the nest.

An albatross and its chick.

Did you know?
In the wild, small birds live for about two to five years. Bigger birds live longer, up to 20 or 30 years. Most wild birds do not die of old age. Millions are killed by animals, such as foxes or rats, or by cars. Others starve when food is short, or die from disease.

Mammal life cycles

Whales, elephants, shrews, bats and humans all belong to a group of animals called **mammals**. Mammals **reproduce sexually**. They feed their babies on milk and care for them until they are old and strong enough to look after themselves. Most mammal babies grow inside their mothers. The babies look like their parents when they are born. But two types of mammals have more unusual life cycles. These mammals are called **monotremes** and **marsupials**.

Laying eggs

Monotremes are mammals that lay eggs. There are only three types of monotremes. They are the duck-billed platypus, the long-beaked echidna and the short-beaked echidna. The platypus lays two eggs in a riverbank tunnel. The echidna lays a single egg. She carries the egg in a small pouch under her body.

A short-beaked echidna.

Kangaroo life cycle

Marsupials are mammals with pouches. Koalas, kangaroos and opossums are all marsupials. A new-born kangaroo is very small and weak. It has to grow bigger and stronger inside its mother's pouch. Here you can see how a baby kangaroo grows.

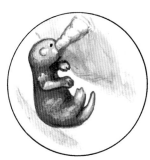

1 The new-born kangaroo is tiny. It crawls up its mother's fur and into her pouch.

2 Inside the pouch, the baby grips a teat. It drinks milk and grows.

3 After six months, the baby leaves the pouch for the first time. But it soon hops back in again.

4 The baby leaves the pouch for good when it is about nine months old. It may live for 15 to 20 years.

Did you know?

The Virginia opossum is a marsupial from North America. Its babies are born after just eight to thirteen days. The baby spends four to five weeks in its mother's pouch. The opossum has the most babies of any mammal, with about 20 in a litter.

More mammal babies

Most mammal babies grow inside their mothers' bodies until they are ready to be born. They grow in their mother's **womb**. The babies look like small versions of their parents. These mammals are called **placental** mammals. As the baby grows inside its mother, it gets **oxygen** and food from her. At the same time the mother takes waste products from the baby. When the baby is born, its mother feeds it on milk and looks after it until it can care for itself.

A horse **suckling** her foal.

Blue whale babies

Blue whale babies are born underwater. They have to come to the surface to breathe. So baby whales are born tail first to stop them drowning as they are being born. Their mothers push them to the surface to take their first breath. A blue whale baby is huge. When it is born, it is 6 to 8 metres long and weighs a whopping 2 to 3 tonnes. It drinks 200 litres (a small bathtub-full) of its mother's milk every day.

Batty nurseries

Free-tailed bats look after their young inside caves where they are safe and warm. The caves are dark and very crowded. One cave may hold ten million baby bats. At night, the females leave the cave to look for food. When they return, they can find their own baby in the crowd by its call and smell.

Baby faces

All mammals care for their babies. The way a baby mammal looks often shows that it needs looking after. A baby orang-utan is small, with big eyes and jerky movements. This tells the adult orang-utans that it is a baby and needs special care.

A baby orang-utan.

Did you know?

A tiny shrew only lives for twelve to eighteen months. It is born one year and it dies the next. A huge elephant lives to be 55 to 70 years old. The oldest elephant ever lived to the grand old age of 82 years.

Human life cycles

Like baby whales, orang-utans and bats, human babies grow inside their mothers' bodies. When the baby is born, its mother feeds it on milk and takes care of it. Human parents look after their young for many years.

How a baby grows

For nine months, the mother carries the baby in the **womb**. Here you can see how the baby grows.

  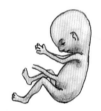  

Month 1 – The baby's heart begins to beat.

Month 2 – The baby has hands and feet.

Month 3 – The baby's body is fully formed.

Month 4 – The baby grows hair and nails.

Month 5 – The baby grows quickly.

 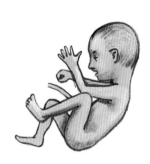  

Month 6 – The baby sleeps and wakes up at set times.

Month 7 – The baby moves about. Its lungs work now.

Month 8 – The baby sucks its thumb, ready to suck milk.

Month 9 – The baby turns head down, ready to be born.

A baby begins

A baby is made from an **egg cell** from its mother and a **sperm** cell from its father. The sperm **fertilizes** the egg to make a new cell. The new **cell** divides to make a ball of cells. Then it sticks to the lining of the mother's womb and starts to grow into a baby.

Growing up

Your body grows until you are about 20 years old. During that time, it goes through many changes. Your bones get longer and make you taller. Your muscles get stronger. Between the ages of eleven and thirteen, your body starts to change from a child into an adult. This is called **puberty**. Girls grow breasts and start to have **periods**. Boys grow hair on their bodies and their voices get deeper.

Growing old

At about 60 to 70 years old, people begin to look older. Their bodies change. It takes longer to repair wear and tear. Their skin gets wrinkled and they may stoop when they stand up. Their hair may turn white or grey. But if people take care of themselves, they can live for many more years.

Conclusion

Living things are always being born and dying. Nature's life cycles are going on all the time. They are often linked to the seasons. In winter, nature is barren and bare. In spring, many plants start to bloom and animals have their babies. New life is created and a new life cycle begins.

Glossary

asexual a type of reproduction. It only needs one parent. The parent splits in two, or part of the parent splits or buds off, to make a new living thing.

cap the round top of a mushroom or toadstool

cell a tiny building block that makes up the body of all living things

chemical a substance found as a solid, liquid or gas

chick a baby bird

egg cell a special cell made by a female animal. It joins with a male sperm to make a new living thing. It is also called an ovum.

fertilization when a male sperm cell joins a female egg cell to make a new cell. The new cell grows into a new living thing.

fresh fresh water is not salty

germination the way in which a seed grows into a new plant

gills 1) ridges under a mushroom's or toadstool's cap. Spores grow on the ridges. 2) Part of a fish's or young amphibian's body used for breathing in oxygen from water.

iodine a type of chemical

larva the young of an insect. A larva does not look anything like an adult insect.

mammal an animal such as an elephant, bat, horse and human. They are the only animals that feed their babies on milk.

marsupial a mammal that has a pouch in which its baby grows

mate 1) a partner to produce young with. 2) To reproduce.

metamorphosis the way in which an insect's body changes as it grows from an egg into an adult.

mineral a substance that helps build up a living thing's body and keep it healthy

monotreme a mammal that lays eggs

nectar a sweet, sugary liquid made inside a flower. Bees and butterflies visit a flower to drink the nectar. While they are drinking, their bodies get covered in pollen for pollination.

nymph the young of an insect. A nymph looks like a small version of an adult insect.

ovule the special female part of a plant. An ovule joins with male pollen to make a seed. The seed grows into a new plant.

oxygen a gas in the air. Living things need to breathe oxygen to stay alive.

period a small amount of blood which comes from a woman's body once a month. It happens if she makes an egg and the egg is not fertilized.

photosynthesis the way green plants make their own food from sunlight, carbon dioxide and water

placental mammals whose babies grow inside their mothers' bodies until they are ready to be born

pollen tiny grains of powder that are the special male parts of a plant. Pollen joins with a female ovule to make a seed. The seed grows into a new plant.

pollination the way pollen is carried from a male flower to a female flower or from the male part of a flower to the female part

puberty a time in a boy's or girl's life when their bodies change from being a child to being an adult

pupa a stage in an insect's life cycle. Inside the pupa, or case, the insect's body changes into an adult.

reproduction how living things make more of themselves

sexual a type of reproduction. It needs two parents, one male and one female. Each makes special cells which must join together to make a new cell. The new cell grows into a new living thing.

sperm special cells made by a male animal. A sperm joins with a female egg cell to make a new living thing.

spores tiny, dust-like specks of living material. Some plants grow from spores.

suckling drinking milk

tadpole a stage in an amphibian's life cycle. Tadpoles look like tiny fish.

womb part of a female mammal's body in which a baby grows

yolk yellow part of an egg

Index